From the Battlefields of France to Arlington National Cemetery

The Unknown Soldier's Journey Home

Written by Nancy Rust and Carol Stubbs
Illustrated by Melissa Vandiver

Acadian House
PUBLISHING

On the Cover – *Pulled by six black horses, the flag-draped casket of the Unknown Soldier makes its way to the Rotunda of the U.S. Capitol in Washington, D.C., on November 10, 1921. There, a stream of people from every walk of life would come to pay their respects, many of them with tears in their eyes, many of them bearing flowers.*

The Acadian House Publishing Speaker's Bureau can bring authors to your live event. For more information or to book an author, contact Acadian House Publishing at (337) 235-8851, Ext. 104, or info@acadianhouse.com.

Library of Congress Number: 2021943739

ISBN-10: 1-7352641-8-0
ISBN-13: 978-1-7352641-8-9

• Published by Acadian House Publishing, Lafayette, Louisiana (Edited by
  Madison Louviere; Trent Angers, co-editor; pre-press production by Allison Nassans)
• Cover illustration by Melissa Vandiver, New Orleans, Louisiana
• Printed by Walsworth Printing, Marceline, Missouri

*With gratitude to all who
serve and all who wait*

Everyone thought the War to End All Wars would be the last war ever fought. They thought it would be over quickly. They were wrong.

World War I lasted four long years – from 1914 to 1918. Over thirty countries fought in this war. Americans went overseas to fight, too. When the fighting finally ended, soldiers went home to their families and friends.

Many of them did not return. Many had died in battle. Soldiers who died in battle were usually buried on battlegrounds. Sometimes their identification tags were lost. If no one knew who they were, they were called unknown soldiers.

Americans were happy the war was over, but they were very sad that many soldiers had not returned. How could they honor these soldiers?

Hamilton Fish III had an idea. He had been an officer with the famed Harlem Hellfighters. After the war, he was elected to the United States House of Representatives. So he presented his idea to Congress. He wanted to bring home and honor one American unknown soldier.

He said the unknown soldier would represent all soldiers. The soldier would represent every son, brother, husband, and father who fought and died in the war. Congress agreed.

Captain Graves Erskine was entrusted to bring this unknown soldier home from a battlefield in France. Captain Erskine, a Marine from Louisiana, had fought in the war and had been wounded. He had spent more than a year recovering from his injuries. But when he was given this assignment, he was ready. He and thirty-eight Marines boarded the *USS Olympia* in Virginia. On October 14, 1921, the ship landed in England. The sailors and Marines participated in parades and ceremonies to honor the British Unknown Soldier. After nine days, the *Olympia* left England.

The next day, the *Olympia* landed in Le Havre, France.

In France, special ceremonies were held to honor the American Unknown Soldier. On October 25, Captain Erskine and the other men on the *Olympia* stood on the deck. They watched as the caisson bearing the Unknown Soldier rolled into the harbor. American and French soldiers walked beside the flag-draped casket. It was a moment Captain Erskine would never forget. People lined the streets to watch. Church bells rang. White roses lay on top of the casket. They were a gift from a French family who had lost two sons in the war.

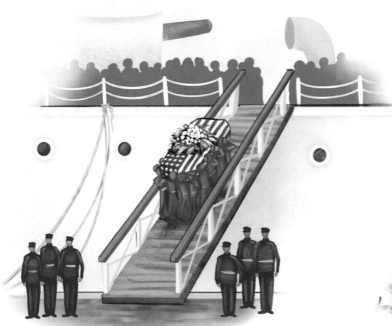

Six sailors and two Marines carried the Unknown Soldier onto the *Olympia*. The ship's band played the French and American national anthems. French citizens and school children laid more flowers on the casket. The visitors left the ship, and the gangplank was removed.

The Marines placed the casket on the bridge of the ship. The ship's carpenters built a wooden frame to protect it. Sailors covered it and tied it down to hold it secure in rough seas.

14

A seventeen-gun salute rang out as the ship
left the harbor. The journey home began.

On the ship, Marines guarded the Unknown Soldier every second of every day – through bright sun and heavy rain. On the sixth day, a terrifying storm swept across the sea. The ship rolled and creaked. Winds howled and drowned out voices. Gigantic waves crashed into the ship and washed over the deck. Men tied themselves with ropes to keep from being swept overboard. Marines struggled to protect the Unknown Soldier. Sailors fought to keep the ship afloat. Storms raged for days.

The seas were still rough when the crew sighted the Cape Henry lighthouse at Chesapeake Bay.

A light rain fell as the ship reached Washington, D.C. The Third Cavalry waited on the cobblestone dock to take charge of the Unknown Soldier. The casket was placed on another caisson drawn by six black horses. The procession made its way to the Rotunda of the United States Capitol.

The next day, the Rotunda opened to the public. All through the day and far into the night, an unending stream of people walked in silence by the casket. Mothers carrying babies. Limping veterans. Boys with caps in hand. Men in suits and men in threadbare coats. Women in furs. Girls in hand-sewn dresses. From every corner of America they came with flowers to honor the Unknown Soldier.

22

On the eleventh hour of the eleventh day of the eleventh month in 1921, the Unknown Soldier made one last journey. Crowds filled the streets. Many wept openly as the caisson moved slowly through the streets of Washington, D.C., over the Potomac River and into Arlington National Cemetery.

At the cemetery, President Harding presented the Medal of Honor. He said the Unknown Soldier "might have come from any one of millions of American homes."

Chief Plenty Coups, representing Native Americans, lifted his arms and prayed. He removed his war bonnet. He laid it and a coup stick on the casket. Many countries honored the Unknown Soldier with their highest medals.

The Unknown Soldier was placed in a marble tomb. He was buried with soil from a battlefield in France and with the white roses from the French family.

25

The War to End All Wars was not the last war. It is now called World War I. Since then, there have been more wars and more unknown soldiers.

Sentinels guard them hour after hour, day after day. Through hurricanes. In blizzards. On sunny days and stormy nights. The Unknown Soldiers are never alone.

Every year, millions of people visit this national monument. They come to mourn and honor these heroes. Many bring flowers. Many bring white roses, like the first roses placed on the casket of the Unknown Soldier.

For the centennial year, the Ducher family, the French family who gave the white roses to the first Unknown Soldier, unveiled another gift for the American people. They created a new variety of white rose named Never Forget. Across America, Never Forget gardens are growing in remembrance of these fallen soldiers.

Who's Who
(In Order of Appearance)

Congressman Hamilton Fish III was born in 1888 to a prominent New York family. He graduated from Harvard and served in the New York State Assembly before joining the army. He was awarded a Silver Star for his service as an officer with the 369th Infantry Regiment. He served in Congress from 1920 to 1945. He died at age 102 in 1991.

Harlem Hellfighters is the popular name for the 369th Infantry Regiment. Most members of the all-Black regiment were from Harlem. They faced racism in America before deploying to France. They became renowned in battle and experienced more continuous combat than any other American unit of their size, with 191 days in the front-line trenches. The French government awarded the entire regiment the *Croix de Guerre*, but it took years for the American government to honor the men, many posthumously.

General Graves Blanchard Erskine, who was awarded the Purple Heart and Silver Star in WWI, was born in 1897 in Columbia, Louisiana. He graduated from Louisiana State University in 1917 and joined the Marine Corps. He served in World War I, World War II, and the Korean War. He later worked as assistant to four Secretaries of Defense. Erskine Bay in Antarctica is named for him.

USS Olympia is a cruiser that was commissioned in 1895. The *Olympia* served as Admiral George Dewey's flagship during the Battle of Manila Bay in 1898. Her last mission was to transport the Unknown Soldier from France to the Washington Navy Yard. She is now docked at the Independence Seaport Museum in Philadelphia, Pennsylvania.

Chief Plenty Coups was born in 1848 in Montana and grew up in the Crow traditions. As a young man, he proved himself as a valiant warrior, visionary leader, and proficient hunter before serving as a lead scout for the army. In the 1880s, he settled on a ranch and became known as a man of peace whose leadership helped bridge the gap between two cultures.

Ducher Family owns *Roseraie Ducher*, a rose nursery founded in 1845 in Lyon, France, by Claude Ducher. The Pernet-Ducher family lost two sons, Claudius and Georges, in World War I. *Roseraie Ducher* developed the Never Forget rose for the Centennial of the Tomb of the Unknown Soldier.

Important Dates

1845 – Claude Ducher establishes his rose nursery, *Roseraie Ducher*, in Lyon, France.

1848 – Plenty Coups is born in Montana.

1897 – June 28, Graves Erskine is born in Columbia, Louisiana.

1914 – July, World War I begins in Europe.

1915 – May 7, a German U-Boat sinks the British ship *Lusitania* with 128 Americans on board.

1917 – April 2, President Woodrow Wilson calls for war.

1917 – April 6, Congress declares war.

1918 – November 11, a ceasefire comes into effect.

1919 – June 28, the Treaty of Versailles is signed.

1920 – December 21, Hamilton Fish III introduces Tomb of the Unknown Soldier bill in U.S. Congress.

1921 – March 4, Congress approves the Tomb of the Unknown Soldier bill.

1921 – September 28, the *USS Olympia* begins journey to France.

1921 – October 14, the *USS Olympia* arrives in Plymouth, England.

1921 – October 24, the *USS Olympia* arrives in Le Havre, France.

1921 – October 25, the Unknown Soldier is taken aboard the *USS Olympia.*

1921 – October 25, Hurricane 6 makes landfall in Florida before moving into the Atlantic Ocean.

1921 – November 9, the *USS Olympia* docks at Washington Navy Yard.

1921 – November 10, Unknown Soldier lies in state in United States Capitol Rotunda.

1921 – November 11, Unknown Soldier of World War I is buried in Arlington Cemetery.

1922 – December, the *USS Olympia* is retired.

1931 – Marble sarcophagus is installed on top of the Unknown Soldier tomb.

1932 – March 3, Chief Plenty Coups dies in Montana.

1948 – April 6, the Army's 3rd United States Infantry Regiment begins guarding the Tomb of the Unknown Soldier twenty-four hours a day, 365 days a year.

1957 – The *Olympia* becomes part of the Independence Seaport Museum in Philadelphia.

1958 – May 30, Unknown Soldiers of World War II and the Korean War are buried in Arlington Cemetery.

1973 – May 21, General Graves B. Erskine dies in Bethesda, Maryland.

1984 – May 28, Unknown Soldier of Vietnam War is buried in Arlington Cemetery.

1991 – Congressman Hamilton Fish III dies in New York.

1998 – May 14, remains of the Unknown Soldier of Vietnam are exhumed.

1998 – June 30, announcement is made identifying the remains of the Unknown Soldier of Vietnam as those of Michael Blassie.

1999 – September 17, tomb of the Unknown Soldier of Vietnam is re-dedicated to honor all missing service members from the Vietnam War.

2021 – The Ducher family unveils the Never Forget rose for the centennial.

Glossary

Bridge: A platform on a ship where the commander or captain can oversee operations.

Caisson: A two-wheeled cart that was once used to carry ammunition to battle and wounded soldiers away from the battlefield. Now it is used for state and military funerals. The caisson is attached to a limber, a two-wheeled cart drawn by horses.

Cavalry: A military unit that moves quickly. Long ago, the cavalry rode on horseback; now it is an armored vehicle unit.

Casket: A box to hold the body of a deceased person. The Unknown Soldier was placed in a specially designed silver and ebony casket.

Coup Stick: A stick with feathers or fur used by Native Americans to touch an enemy while causing no harm or to count acts of bravery.

Rotunda: A round building or room, usually with a dome. The U.S. Capitol has a rotunda.

Sentinel: A person who stands guard and watches over something.

Dear Reader,

Writing this book was a humbling experience. We were inspired by the detailed preparation to bring the Unknown Soldier from France to America and also by the courageous people directly associated with his journey. Most of all, we were touched by the people from every walk of life who rallied to honor this soldier who is "known but to God." The Unknown Soldier is everyone's soldier with no consideration of heritage, status, or politics.

This history is our history. It's also your history, whoever you are and wherever you may be, for it is the history of a person who left home and fought for a better world. May this history inspire us to walk a path with kindness and respect for all.

– N.R. and C.S.

About the Authors...

Nancy Rust is passionate about books and believes well-chosen words can empower young people and make the world a better place. After nearly three decades of teaching reading, writing, and literature, she sat down with her computer and began her career as an author. She likes to take early morning walks, go on road trips, play word games, and visit other countries. She majored in English at Western Kentucky University and got Master of Arts and Education Specialist degrees from Louisiana State University. She and her husband share their home near Lafayette, Louisiana, with a lively standard poodle named Truman.

Nancy and Carol have written five books together for readers of all ages. You can catch up with them on their Facebook page, Nancy & Carol Books, or learn more about their books and read their blog at www.nancycarolbooks.com.

Carol Stubbs grew up with a love of reading and writing that was encouraged by her family. Her writing career has included being a journalist, freelance writer, English teacher, and author. She is also a potter and enjoys creating designs inspired by Louisiana swamps and bayous. She has a Bachelor of Arts degree from Louisiana State University and a Masters in Education from the University of Louisiana at Lafayette. She is a member of the Louisiana Crafts Guild and the Society of Children's Book Writers and Illustrators. As a part of the Louisiana/Mississippi region, she leads the monthly SCBWI Acadiana Critique Group. She lives in south Louisiana with her husband and two cats, and likes traveling to visit her children and grandchildren.

Since 2011, Nancy and Carol have written five books together for readers of all ages. Learn more about the books at www.nancycarolbooks.com.

About the Artist...

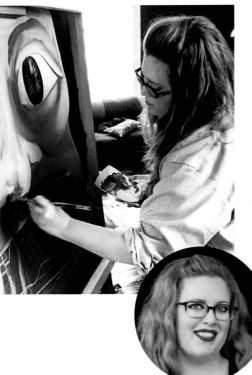

Melissa Vandiver is a New Orleans-based artist and illustrator, specializing in painting and digital art. She studied architecture at Clemson University, and shortly after moved to New Orleans to do Hurricane Katrina relief work. After nearly a decade in architecture-related jobs, she decided to pursue her true passion: art.

Melissa's artistic mission is simple: to create images that evoke joy. This is sometimes through picture books, sometimes comic strips, and sometimes whimsical portraits of animals in costume. When not painting, Melissa can be found playing with glitter or out on the town with a tiny dog.

The Never Forget Rose and Garden

The Never Forget Rose was developed especially for the Centennial commemoration of the Tomb of the Unknown Soldier. It was born in a rose nursery in France called *Roseraie Ducher*. While it may not look quite like the traditional florist rose, it is one of the white roses recognized by the American Rose Society as the official flower of the Centennial of the Unknown Soldier.

– Photo courtesy of Fabien Ducher

A Never Forget Garden that includes this special flower can be cultivated in your own back yard as a living tribute to all U.S. service members who have fought and died for our liberty and freedom. (For information on creating your own Never Forget Garden, go to www.rose.org/never-forget-garden.)

---

4 WAYS TO ORDER additional copies of *The Unknown Soldier's Journey Home...*

• **Online** - Go to www.acadianhouse.com.
• **By phone** - Just call in your order: (800) 850-8851, Ext. 102.
• **By mail** - Send us a note with the title of the book and number of copies you'd like to order, at $14 each. For shipping & handling, add $4 for the first book and $1 for each additional book thereafter. Louisiana residents add 8% tax to the cost of the books. Mail your order and check or credit card authorization (VISA / MC / AmEx / Discover) to: Acadian House Publishing, P.O. Box 52247, Lafayette, LA 70505.
• **Shop local** - Check with your local bookstore or gift shop.